FUTURISTIC ELECTRIC Buses

KERRILY SAPET

Mitchell Lane

PUBLISHERS

2001 SW 31st Avenue
Hallandale, FL 33009
www.mitchelllane.com

Copyright © 2020 by Mitchell Lane Publishers. All rights reserved. No part of this book may be reproduced without written permission from the publisher. Printed and bound in the United States of America.

FUTURISTIC ELECTRIC

First Edition, 2020.
Author: Kerrily Sapet
Designer: Ed Morgan
Editor: Sharon F. Doorasamy

Series: Futuristic Electric
Title: Buses / by Kerrily Sapet

Hallandale, FL : Mitchell Lane Publishers, [2020]

Library bound ISBN: 9781680203486
eBook ISBN: 9781680203493

PHOTO CREDITS: Design Elements, freepik.com, Cover Photo: JACQUES DEMARTHON/AFP/Getty Images, p. 5 Public Domain, p. 6 Lucas Davies on Unsplash, p. 9 Spielvogel CC0 1.0 wikicommons, p. 10 Proterra Inc. CC-BY-SA-4.0 wikicommons, p. 11 Frank Schwichtenberg CC-BY-SA-4.0, p. 15 David Mareuil/Anadolu Agency/Getty Images, p. 17 FRED TANNEAU/AFP/Getty Images, p. 18 SounderBruce CC-BY-SA-2.0, p. 19 freepik.com, p. 27 Domdomegg CC-BY-4.0, p. 21 SanJoaquinRTD CC-BY-SA-3.0, p. 22 MANDEL NGAN/AFP/Getty Images, p. 25 Wahsaw, p. 27 domdomegg CC-BY-4.0

CONTENTS

Chapter One
A CARRIAGE FOR ALL   4

Chapter Two
GOING ELECTRIC   8

Chapter Three
MOTORS IN MOTION   14

Chapter Four
COMING TO A STREET NEAR YOU   20

Chapter Five
LOOKING TO THE FUTURE   24

WHAT YOU SHOULD KNOW   28
GLOSSARY   29
WORKS CONSULTED   30
FURTHER READING   31
ON THE INTERNET   31
INDEX   32
ABOUT THE AUTHOR   32

Words in **bold** throughout can be found in the Glossary.

Chapter One

A CARRIAGE FOR ALL

Cities have always been crowded and dirty. Ancient Romans complained about traffic and pollution 2,000 years ago. Horse-drawn carriages jammed streets long before cars and buses. Horse manure piled up. It stuck to people's shoes and attracted clouds of flies. Streets became busier and smellier as more people moved to cities.

In 1662 in France, Blaise Pascal invented the omnibus—a "carriage for all." While most carriages only held a few people, Pascal's omnibus could seat eight people. This new invention spread to other cities. By the 1800s, double-decker omnibuses, pulled by horses, carried 42 passengers. The word "omnibus" was shortened to "bus."

An invention by Carl Benz changed transportation forever. As Benz rode his bike to school over the muddy hills of his hometown in Germany, he dreamed of an easier way to travel—a "horseless carriage." Benz, like his father, was good at building machines. Benz designed a gas engine and, in 1885, he used it to power the first car. That car looked like a large motorized tricycle. Few people could afford a car though. Gas was only sold at drugstores for cleaning.

Benz looked for other uses for his engine. "The love of inventing never dies," he said. Benz attached the engine to a carriage with seats for eight people and a driver. His invention became the world's first motorized bus. Soon Benz's company was building buses with stronger engines that could go faster and carry more people.

News of Carl Benz's inventions spread fast. Other inventors used the technology in their own designs for cars and buses. They built more powerful engines, better tires, and tougher and safer vehicles. By the 1930s, buses looked much like they do now. There are single buses, double-decker buses, trolley buses, and even buses that link together.

Passengers aboard a bus in Queensland, Australia, around 1930

CHAPTER ONE

London's famous double-decker bus

Billions of people around the world ride buses to work and school. They hop aboard buses to shop and to visit friends. Passengers may travel a few city blocks or thousands of miles. Buses are inexpensive to ride. They carry many people, which lessens traffic. But most buses run on gasoline or diesel fuel, which is made from **fossil fuels**.

A Carriage for All

Fossil fuels are formed from the remains of plants and animals that died millions of years ago. They are a **nonrenewable resource**. Once they're used up, they're gone. Fossil fuels must be burned to make energy. When fossil fuels burn, they release carbon dioxide. A diesel bus releases one pound of carbon dioxide into the air every mile. The carbon dioxide builds up in the Earth's atmosphere. It traps heat from the sun and causes **climate change**.

When engines burn fossil fuels, particulates, tiny pieces of leftover fuel, escape into the air. Particulates may be thinner than a hair, but they add up to billions of tons of air pollution. Breathing polluted air can cause asthma, lung diseases, and other serious health problems.

Air pollution contributes to millions of deaths each year. People around the world are working to stop the pollution caused by buses. Many believe electric buses are the answer.

Fun Facts

1. About 2.4 million people ride the bus every day in New York City.

2. Schools close and people stay inside on days when pollution makes the air unsafe to breathe in some cities.

Chapter Two
GOING ELECTRIC

People on every continent are experimenting with electric vehicles. The first electric buses were slow and couldn't go far. They recharged slowly. Today they go faster and farther than ever. "Electric buses are no longer a science-fair project," says Macy Neshati of BYD, the world's largest electric vehicle maker.

Electric buses offer big advantages over gas or diesel buses. Electric buses run on batteries. They are **zero-emission** vehicles, which means they don't produce pollution. Electric buses use electricity stored in batteries to power a motor. The motor turns the wheels of the bus. Electric motors have fewer moving parts than gas engines, so they are easier to fix. Electricity is cheaper than gas or diesel.

Lithium-ion batteries on a 120 kilowatt electric engine by Winston Battery

Electric buses use rechargeable lithium-ion batteries, the same type of batteries in cell phones and laptops. The batteries can be recharged by plugging the bus in at a charging station. Charging the batteries takes a few hours, about the time it takes to charge an iPad.

Batteries don't have the power of fossil fuels. To equal the driving distance of one pound of a fossil fuel, a battery must weigh 100 pounds. Electric buses have battery packs the size of twin mattresses. The long, flat battery packs line the floors or ceilings of the buses.

CHAPTER TWO

The Proterra E2 Catalyst Max

Proterra, a company in California, builds electric buses, batteries, chargers, and motors. "Our technology could literally remove every single dirty diesel bus from cities," says Ryan Popple of Proterra. Proterra's bus, the Catalyst E2 Max, broke records by going 1,101 miles without recharging. Proterra's buses run routes in cities across the United States. Proterra is also working on a self-driving bus.

BYD, short for "Build Your Dreams," is a Chinese company. BYD has sold electric buses to more than 200 cities. Their factory in California can make 1,500 electric buses each year. BYD is working on a self-driving bus to release by 2020.

Going Electric

Navya's Arma

Navya, a French company, is developing a self-driving electric bus to carry 15 people. Called "Arma," the bus uses sensors to scan and map its surroundings. The Arma could be used for routes that are too crowded for larger buses. Navya is testing the Arma in Paris and London.

GreenPower is one of several companies designing electric school buses. GreenPower's bus looks like a typical yellow school bus but runs on nine batteries. School buses release 90,000 tons of pollution each year. "Electric buses have the benefit of kids not standing around or having their windows open while diesel fumes are being released," says Jeremy Firestone of the University of Delaware. In 2017, California ordered 30 GreenPower school buses.

CHAPTER TWO

Car companies, such as Volvo, Mercedes, and Hyundai, are joining the race to make electric buses. Mercedes-Benz is testing an electric bus in the freezing Arctic Circle and the heat of Spain. Mercedes-Benz is also developing a self-driving bus to be released in 2018.

Companies are also experimenting with biofuels, fuels made from plants. They are testing fuel cells, which combine hydrogen and oxygen to produce electrical energy. One company has made a bus that runs on fuel from food scraps and human waste.

With countless companies exploring greener technology, more electric buses will be hitting the roads.

"If you see an electric bus now, it's a rarity. In 10 years, it will probably be the reverse: If you see a gas or diesel vehicle, [that] will be a rarity."

—JIM REYNOLDS, ADOMANI

Going Electric

Fun Facts

1 An electric bus eliminates 1,690 tons of carbon dioxide and 350 pounds of particulates in 12 years.

2 Kids are more at risk from air pollution because they breathe twice as fast as adults.

When Proterra's founder Dale Hill started out he "didn't know a bus from a wheelbarrow." He hired engineers from car and airplane makers such as Tesla, BMW, and Cessna, and a NASCAR engine building team. Building electric buses takes experts working together. Hill sees Proterra as part of the pollution solution.

Chapter Three

MOTORS IN MOTION

Electric buses look like gas or diesel buses on the outside. Under the hood, they're not the same at all. Electric motors work differently than gas engines. A gas engine moves by creating tiny explosions. The explosions push metal parts connected to the **driveshaft**, which turns the wheels. In an electric motor, the motor and the driveshaft don't touch. The driveshaft is pushed magnetically. Electric motors are "a very beautiful, efficient thing," says Dustin Grace, who designs electric motors.

The self-driving bus Arma on its first test drive on a public road in Tokyo, Japan, in December 2007

Electric motors are more powerful at lower speeds than gas engines. They deliver more **torque**, a turning force. "Torque is what you need to get a car going," says Grace, who is vice president of engineering, energy storage, and power systems at Proterra Inc. Electric motors speed up faster than gas engines because batteries deliver power instantly. Electric motors also feed themselves electricity. When drivers put on the brakes, the motor runs in reverse, sending electricity back into the battery.

Electric motors have one moving part. Gas engines have hundreds of parts. Engineers can redesign the spaces in electric buses because the motors are small. The motor in an electric bus can be lifted by one person.

"Our buses are designed from day one as electric vehicles," says Brendan Riley of GreenPower. "Instead of taking existing bus designs and fitting everything in them, we draw the battery and electric motor first, and then build the bus around that."

CHAPTER THREE

Engineers also think about the amount of electricity a battery can store. Electricity is measured in **watts**. A kilowatt-hour is the power supplied by 1,000 watts for one hour. Leaving a light on all day uses one kilowatt-hour. The batteries in Proterra's record-breaking bus store 660 kilowatt-hours.

Batteries don't run as well in cold weather. Engineers are designing heating systems to keep batteries warm when it's cold. Batteries also are heavy. Heavy vehicles take more energy to move. Engineers are solving the problem by building buses with lightweight **composite** materials, mixtures of different materials.

Battery scientists are working to invent smaller, more powerful batteries. Scientists at Argonne National Laboratory have studied more than 22,500 ingredients for new batteries. "When Thomas Edison was trying to develop a light bulb, he tried thousands of different materials . . . to see which ones worked," says Dr. Kyeongjae Cho of the University of Texas.

Motors in Motion

Lithium batteries of the BlueBus, the first electric-bus manufacturer to have 50 vehicles in circulation in France

CHAPTER THREE

King County Metro Transit in Seattle, Washington, plans to add 120 battery-electric buses to its fleet by 2020.

Companies designing electric buses are developing original parts and improved electronics. "If you tell your engineering group one of the rules they have to stick by is they have to use all the old parts from the parts bin, you're going to end up with a terrible product," says Ryan Popple of Proterra. Electric buses feature more electronics than gas or diesel buses. They are giant, battery-powered computers on wheels.

Motors in Motion

Companies around the world are building and testing electric buses. Engineers are using new technology in their designs. Many companies plan for their electric buses to be driving down the streets by 2018. Self-driving buses may be coming as soon as late 2018.

Fun Facts

1. The oldest known battery was invented in Iraq 2,000 years ago.

2. An average bus weighs about as much as two elephants.

Chapter Four

COMING TO A STREET NEAR YOU

Designers are building electric buses in all shapes and sizes. Many companies are building **prototypes**—new models—that cut down on pollution and feature new technologies. Most of the prototypes can even drive themselves.

"If more and more people eat, sleep, and work in cities, a number of big challenges emerge. One major challenge is to move all of these people and to move them fast, safely, and comfortably."

—WOLFGANG BERNHARD, DAIMLER TRUCKS AND BUSES

Proterra is testing a self-driving bus in Reno, Nevada. Proterra is fitting buses with cameras and sensors to track distant objects and sense pedestrians by heat. "The goal is to make sure that it's still a bus," says Popple. "We don't think we'll have too much luck selling a hover bus or something like that at this point." Proterra is also working on fast-charging technology to charge buses in 10 minutes. Dale Hill of Proterra predicts buses in the future will be charged by solar power.

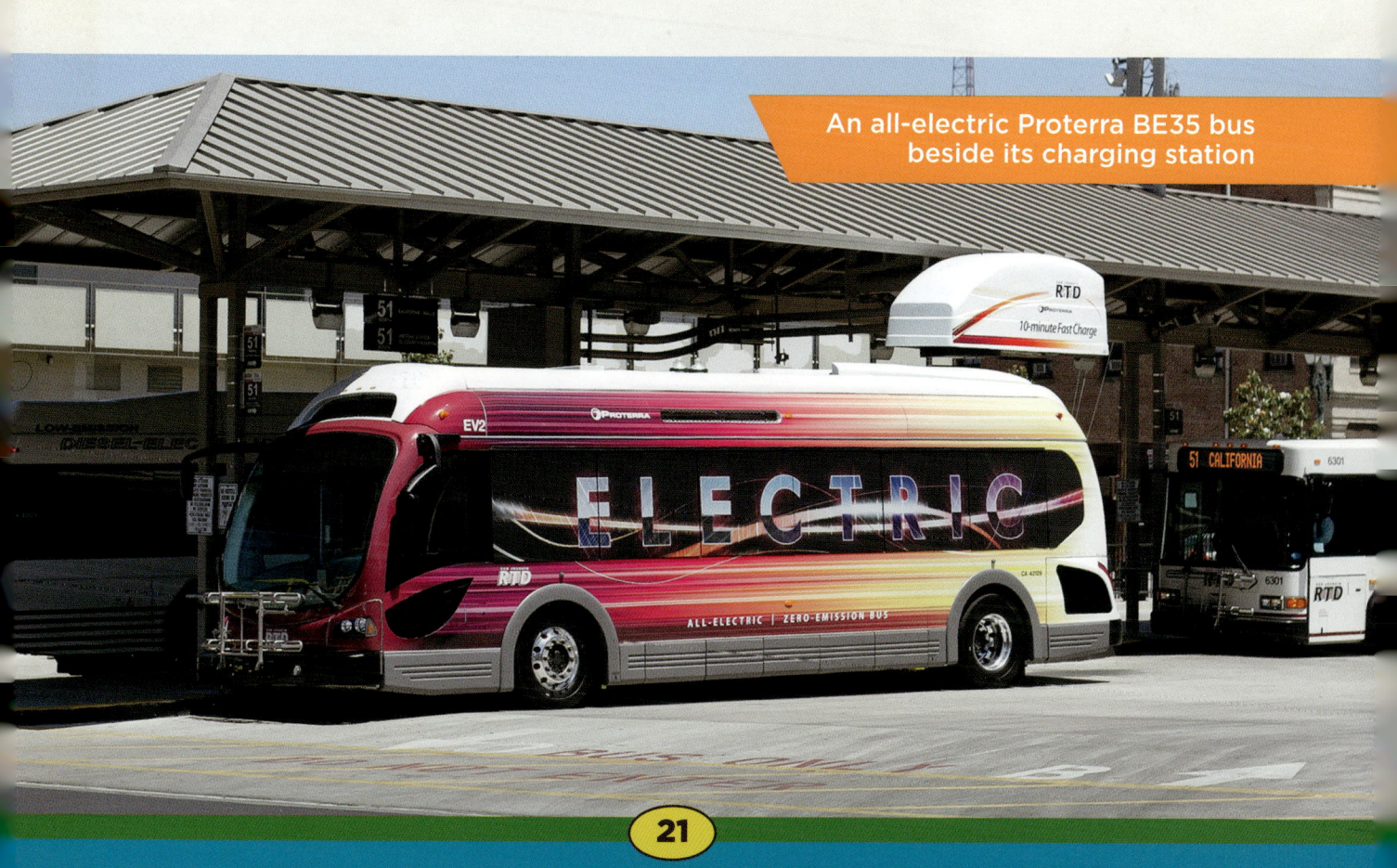

An all-electric Proterra BE35 bus beside its charging station

CHAPTER FOUR

CRCC, a Chinese company, is working on an electric vehicle called "ART." ART is part bus and part train. Its rubber wheels run on the road like a bus. Its cars connect like a train. Each car can hold 100 people. ART follows white lines painted on the road and uses sensors to avoid obstacles. ART is being tested in Zhuzhou, China.

Navya's bus, Arma, can go 28 miles per hour. It is undergoing testing at the University of Michigan's M City, a track built for self-driving vehicles. The company plans to build 150 of the buses by the end of 2018.

Local Motors's self-driving electric bus, called "Olli," carries 12 passengers. Olli uses computer software that allows riders to ask Olli questions about the route, the weather, and nearby attractions. Parts of Olli are printed with a 3D printer. Local Motors is testing Olli in cities throughout the United States. They hope to build thousands of Ollis by 2020.

Olli, the electric self-driving shuttle, is the result of a partnership between Local Motors and IBM, using IBM's Watson supercomputer.

Coming to a Street Near You

Many companies are building electric buses and rolling them out in cities around the world. New exciting prototypes feature technology that is good for the planet. The designs may change how people move from one place to another.

Fun Fact

Electric buses in Seoul, South Korea, are nicknamed "Peanut Buses" because of their shape.

A TRIP TO M CITY

M CITY, AT THE UNIVERSITY OF MICHIGAN, HAS TRAFFIC JAMS, BRIDGES, TUNNELS, HIGHWAY ENTRANCES, AND WALKERS. BUT M CITY ISN'T A REAL CITY. THE MINI CITY WAS BUILT TO EXPERIMENT WITH SELF-DRIVING CARS. SEBASTIAN, A ROBOT, EVEN STEPS OUT INTO TRAFFIC TO MAKE SURE THE SELF-DRIVING CARS HIT THE BRAKES.

THE FUTURE

Imagine a school bus quietly pulling up to a stop. Picture city streets lined with clean, green buses. Think about hopping onto a small bus that talks. You are imagining the near future.

People around the world are excited about electric buses. Many of today's electric buses can travel at highway speeds and go hundreds of miles between charges. They charge at bus stations, plugged in like cell phones, or at overhead charging stations along the bus route. One of Proterra's buses charges in less than 13 minutes.

A Shenzhen bus

The city of Shenzhen in China has 16,359 electric buses. Those buses will decrease carbon dioxide emissions in Shenzhen by 1,350,000 tons a year. Electric buses are operating in more than 200 cities. Within the next seven years, nearly half of all city buses could be electric.

CHAPTER FIVE

Many cities in the United States, Europe, and Asia have promised to cut fossil-fuel powered transportation by 2030. "Human beings can move quickly," says Eric Garcetti, the mayor of Los Angeles. "We can do this." Cities are trying to make the switch to electric buses. An electric bus is more expensive to buy but saves money in fuel and repair costs. "The cash savings for a city of hundreds of thousands of dollars over the bus life," says Popple of Proterra. "That's why we're beating fossil fuel—we're clean, quiet, green, cool, high tech—AND CHEAPER."

Cities are slowly replacing their noisy gas-guzzling buses with quiet zero-emission electric buses. In January 2018, New York City started testing 10 electric buses. The city plans to order 60 more. Los Angeles is replacing more than 2,000 of its buses with electric buses. Each electric bus will help cut back on the air pollution threatening people and the planet.

"No doubt, electric buses are the future of bus transportation," says Jerome Lutin of the NJ Transit.

Looking to the Future

A fully electric-powered double-decker bus in London

Fun Facts

1 The world's first electric double-decker bus was launched in London in 2016.

2 People in many countries check air pollution levels using apps on their phones.

What You Should Know

- In 1662, Blaise Pascal invented the omnibus.
- In 1885, Carl Benz designed the first motorized vehicle.
- When fossil fuels burn, they release carbon dioxide and particulates, causing air pollution.
- Companies around the world are designing and selling electric buses.
- Many companies are testing prototypes for self-driving electric buses.

Glossary

climate change
Change in the Earth's weather patterns caused by pollution

composite
A mix of two or more different materials

driveshaft
The parts of a vehicle that move the wheels

fossil fuels
Fuel formed over millions of years from the remains of plants and animals

nonrenewable resource
A natural supply that cannot be replaced after it is used

prototype
A new design or model

torque
The force that causes turning

watts
A measure of electricity

zero-emission
Refers to an engine, motor, or process that does not produce harmful gas or pollution

Works Consulted

Cooney, Scott. "Interview with Ryan Popple." *Clean Technica*, August 27, 2016.

Dale Hill, interview by author, February 2018.

The website of Mercedes-Benz, accessed March 11, 2016, http://www.Mercedes-Benz.com.

Mitchell, Russ. "Electric-bus Startup Proterra Shifts into Higher Gear." *Los Angeles Times,* June 5, 2017.

Morris, David Z. "Tesla Veteran Explains How Electric Motors Crush Gas Engines." *Fortune*, November 17, 2015.

Pittman, Kagan. "USA Amps Up their Pure-Electric Vehicle Game." Engineering.com, September 8, 2015.

Scauzillo, Steve. "LA Metro Commits to 100% Electric Buses." *San Gabriel Valley Tribune*, July 28, 2017.

Schlosser, Nicole. "Can Electric School Buses Go the Distance?" *School Bus Fleet*, May 23, 2016.

Thompson, Cadie. "Mercedes Created the Bus of the Future." *Business Insider*, June 11, 2017.

University of Delaware. "Diesel Bus Alternative." *Science Daily*, May 29, 2014.

Uhler, Andy. "The Market for Electric Buses is Speeding Right Along." *Marketplace*, June 30, 2017.

Further Reading

Amstutz, L. J. *How Can We Reduce Transportation Pollution?* Minneapolis, MN: Lerner Publications Company, 2016.

Flounders, Anne. *Getting from Here to There.* Concord, MA: Red Chair Press, 2014.

Williams, Brian. *Transportation Technology.* Mankato, MN: Black Rabbit Books, 2009.

On the Internet

http://amhistory.si.edu/onthemove/
A website of the Smithsonian National Museum of American History

http://climatekids.nasa.gov
This kid-friendly website is sponsored by NASA's Jet Propulsion Laboratory / California Institute of Technology

http://www3.epa.gov/airnow/k1/k1.html
An interactive webpage by the U.S. Environmental Protection Agency

Index

batteries 8, 9, 10, 11, 15, 16, 18, 19
Benz, Carl 4, 5
BYD 8, 10
China 22, 25
fossil fuels 6, 7, 9, 26
Grace, Dustin 14, 15
GreenPower 11, 15
Hill, Dale 13, 21
motor 8, 10, 14, 15
Navya 11, 22
particulates 7, 13
Pascal, Blaise 4
pollution 4, 7, 8, 11, 13, 20, 26, 27
Popple, Ryan 10, 18, 21, 26
Proterra 10, 13, 15, 16, 18, 21, 24, 26
prototypes 20, 23

About the Author

KERRILY SAPET is the author of 18 nonfiction books and many magazine articles for kids. This is her second book for Mitchell Lane Publishers. Kerrily has toured New York City and Paris by bus, traveled across states on Greyhound buses, ridden city buses, and spent hours on school buses. She enjoyed learning about cleaner, greener buses. Kerrily currently lives in Illinois with her husband and two sons.